RANDOM THOUGHTS

WHEN YOUR HEAD IS FULL

James O. Anastasi

For information on talks, workshops or to order books, write:

Health Esteem Publishing Company
5506 Lakeview Drive
Clear Lake, Iowa 50428
Phone: 641-423-4180

Visit our website at: www.anastasicounseling.com

ISBN: 978-0-9886460-0-1

First edition: December 2012

PRINTED IN THE UNITED STATES OF AMERICA

Cover photo, a reflection of autumn leaves on the surface of Clear Lake, Iowa, was taken by the author near his home.

Dedicated to my family, past, present and future.

TOPICS

Beliefs
Thoughts
Feelings
Ideas
Politics
Religion
Physical Health
Mental Health
Relationships
Marriage
Parenting
Goals
Fantasy
Vacation
Questions
Curiosities
Challenges
Observations
Everything Else

Other books by the author:
Strategies for Change: Tools for people and for those who help them improve their lives

FORWARD

As a therapist, I obviously talk with people regularly about their beliefs, thoughts, feelings, and behaviors. I hear about their successes and failures, hopes and dreams. I also hear about their disappointments, hopelessness, depression and despair. I hear their explanations of why their relationships flourished or floundered; how their relationships enhanced or diminished their significance and respect. I hear what has and what hasn't worked in their role as parents and in their relationships with God. I hear a lot and think a lot. I also want to share with them what I think may be helpful.

This book is truly random from its conception. I began writing my beliefs and thoughts that I would commonly share with clients and with participants in workshop presentations. I would occasionally write an idea that was thought or heard during the day that resonated in my head until evening. Time alone without an agenda or schedule are times that I would often write random thoughts that were flitting ideas or recalled clichés that were heard throughout my life. I recorded personal observations, impressions of my life experiences, and questions my creativity wouldn't leave alone. The vast majority of the random thoughts are simply that—random thoughts that I expressed when my head was full.

Some of the Random Thoughts are someone else's sayings or clichés that I have used therapeutically or found personally fitting within my own belief system. Where they came from originally, I don't know. I wrote no direct quotes (that I know of) from someone else's writing. There are statements that clients have made that I would add to my collection of thoughts. Because of confidentiality, their names are protected; their permission and input is greatly appreciated.

Pieces of scratch paper were occasionally given to my office manager, Linda Sweeney, who would type and add them to the list. Her ability to interpret scribble is remarkable and greatly appreciated.

My daughter, Angela Swain, was more than helpful and appreciated with her typing and editing assistance. I cannot thank her enough.

Encouragement, insight and editing were provided by Jane Reynolds, Managing Editor of the *Mason City Globe Gazette*. John Skipper, also of the *Mason City Globe Gazette* and Jim Collision, founder of Employers of America, were also supportive and encouraging. Dave Kisilewski, friend and colleague, provided professional insight and editing. My sister,

Carol Keller, was an original reader and gave meaningful support. You are all appreciated.

I am grateful to David Evans of the Laurens House of Print who enabled my ideas to come to printed form. Most helpful and patient was Connie Reinert, owner of Beyond Broken, to whom I am forever grateful for her encouragement, support, insight, creativity and expertise in the final editing and formatting of this project. Thank you.

Greatly appreciated are the thousands of clients and workshop participants who, in a state of vulnerability and with naive trust, have shared their lives with me. Their confidence in me is humbling. I hope they have continued to benefit and grow. I thank them for their ideas, inspiration, and wisdom.

My family of origin, including grandparents, aunts, uncles, and cousins, has provided material enough for several books. My parents and siblings continue to be an ongoing inspiration.

I am most grateful to my wife, best friend and most avid supporter, Kathy. I am also grateful to our three daughters and son-in-laws, Miquel and Kevin Melchert, Angela and John Swain, and Cara and Owen Margherio; and five grandchildren, Madison, Lexis, and Samantha Swain, and Cooper and Cambri Melchert. They are my greatest love and inspiration.

RANDOM THOUGHTS

If I take personally everything that is said to me I will truly be one confused individual.

If I emphasize the good of any situation and minimize the not-so-good, I can make any situation a pleasant experience.

Snow days are days of irresponsibility with a good excuse.

I'm continuously amazed at the relaxation that is felt when in an environment where there is no opportunity to be responsible.

Thinking that I'm almost perfect puts a unique perspective on life as I know it to be.

If emotions can be controlled by thought, why do so many people think the thoughts that cause them pain?

Love is the experience that enables two totally different beings to appreciate their differences rather than attempt to change the other to be more like them.

The greatest statistic is that there is an exception.

The only statistics I care to know are the ones that are true and the ones that are not true. The rest aren't worth my time.

If beauty was only skin deep, there would be a lot of ugly people in the world. As it is, most people are quite attractive.

If you are going to walk for exercise, you might as well go someplace. Going in circles seems a little redundant and can become vicious.

Does longevity make a happy life or does a happy life make longevity?

Some of the most pleasant days are those that are so bad that you can't do anything else.

An easy way of burning calories is to stay cold.

When I die, I hope people will get together and enjoy each other. Then my life and death will have had purpose.

The value of life for the most discouraged seems to be determined by their frame of mind at any given moment.

Finding joy in any situation is probable if you believe it exists.

The value of life is too often not appreciated until the value of life has been diminished.

Those who have little tend to paint what they have more colorfully.

One of the greatest aspects of being on vacation is the realization that you are looking forward to going home.

It's refreshing to find yourself feeling closer to your wife after you've been alone with her.

If I had the choice of eating great food that I spent hours preparing or eating boring food that took little time to prepare, you probably wouldn't want to have supper with me.

Poker is one of those games where you can have the worst hand and still win. That's why I like it.

Walking in snow and walking a soft, sandy beach have more in common than not. In both cases, the walking takes great effort and the scenery makes it worthwhile.

The more time I spend alone, the more I crave spending time alone.

If people were to live where the money is we would all be living in Finland.

Ever wonder what couples who don't talk to each other in restaurants think about?

Never go on an extended vacation to a rental property without someone who likes to cook.

Vacationing in a novel area is seldom disappointing because there are few expectations.

After complaining, "I just played the worst golf game of my life," my friend wanted to encourage me. "You've played worse," he said.

As I get older, I become more narrow-minded regarding narrow-mindedness.

Stress is our body's response to our perception of an event, not the event itself.

Emotion is not good or bad, only the aftermath of our thoughts.

The best stress management technique is to remove the ultimatums from our vocabulary.

It is possible to be highly competent, extremely busy, extraordinarily successful and be stress-free.

If peace can be found in a can of beer then the epicenter of world peace is Madison, Wisconsin, on a Saturday when the Badgers play the Hawkeyes.

If all the money spent on arenas, wages, wagers, and by the spectators, advertisers and promoters along with all of the energy, discussion, and enthusiasm of sporting events was spent on the poor of the world, would there be any hungry children at night?

I care about you. I don't take care of you.

Although there is much more to mental health than positive thinking, positive thinking would improve the mental health of the majority of us.

There is a difference between positive thinking and thinking effectively.

I think Pollyanna really was on to something.

My first cup of coffee must be like the first worm for an early bird.

Has there ever been a "just war"?

All wars seem to be fought over money, territory, religion, power or revenge initiated by immature, unstable people.

If you live on a boat to get away from people, don't moor in a marina.

Never be the expert the first week on the job.

Cooking by a recipe is not nearly as exciting as just making something up. You make a choice between good taste and excitement.

If you want cooperation and good will, don't get an attitude.

If you have the option of buying a boat and inviting your friends on board or having friends with boats and them inviting you onboard, it's best to have friends with boats.

Bad weather on vacation is better than good weather while at work.

The best thing about singing the blues is that if you know the first line you already know the second.

What a blessing to be married to the same woman for over forty years and she still turns your head.

It's not that I have problems that bothers me. What bothers me is I don't have the solutions.

It is often cheaper and wiser to change your perception of your situation than to change the situation.

If you choose to change your situation, your life will be different—not necessarily better.

Wearing a jacket on a chilly day makes a chilly day as nice as a warm day.

The best year of my life is this year. The next best year was last year. My tenth best year was a decade ago.

One of the greatest obstacles to growth is habit.

The biggest difference between successful people and unsuccessful people is that successful people focus on the solutions and unsuccessful people focus on the problems.

I refuse to let my past destroy my future. I will welcome my future learning from my past.

The reason you can't find happiness by searching your surroundings is because it exists in your head.

It is in the state of relaxation that our spirit gets excited.

My body may not know the difference between anxiety and excitement but I sure do.

Once a need is met it is no longer a need and therefore is no longer motivational.

There is a huge difference between being honest and being open.

People who believe, "I'll be happy when . . ." will never be happy.

I would hate to be the kid who was born to make mom happy.

The happiest people are those who decide to not think about unhappiness.

An addiction is a desperate attempt to find happiness outside of myself with continuous failure.

When I think a thought it comes alive. The more I think it the bigger it grows.

Whenever I play solitaire it seems Mom helps me a lot. She died 10 years ago.

The gentlest of giants are whales.

My Dad taught me never to be an addict to anything. He keeps me on the straight and narrow. He died in 1994.

Your relationship with people you love doesn't end with death. It only takes on a new dimension.

Fossil fuel is what we use until we learn of the willingness of nature to provide for us.

If it wasn't for gravity, everything would be up in the air.

If all the energy spent on the negative radio and TV talk shows could be directed toward creating hope, our economy would be experiencing its greatest rally.

The best part of going to parades is watching the people who come to parades.

The gentleness of men is most obvious when with their infants.

When walking an isolated beach in a foreign country, walk less than half the distance that you have energy and water to walk because the walk back is a little further.

The water for kayaking cannot be too rough until you get hurt.

People are about as friendly as you are.

The more stimulated we become, the more dependent we become upon stimulation.

The more overstimulated we become, the more oblivious we become to the subtleties of life.

Do palm trees really release a chemical that relaxes people?

You can tell who lives in the area where you vacation. They are the ones who are dressed appropriately for the weather conditions and typically aren't sunburned.

When I was younger, the places I enjoyed the most were where everyone else was. Today the places I enjoy the most are where there are few.

Why is it that the objects that are considered the most treasured are those that are the least abundant? Does economics have to determine what is considered a treasure?

If you could will one emotion for everyone, what would it be? What one quality? What one belief?

Part of the excitement of foreign travel is not being able to speak the native language. Part of the embarrassment is the inability to respect others by speaking their language.

If I ate till I was full, I would not live long.

Being thin would be easier if I was a picky eater who didn't like carbohydrates.

Life is enjoyable even with difficult people. Life is easier to enjoy with pleasant people.

Few pleasures are more soothing than skin contact.

Complete stops at stop signs, when no one is coming, are only necessary in legalistic cultures with too many attorneys.

Entrepreneurship is norm in developing countries.

Life becomes more structured and planned when you don't have a car.

The surest means to a smile is to hear the joy of a child.

If you want to be found in a crowd wear a good looking hat.

The poorer the people, the closer they live to one another. Is there a message there?

Every home should have a wind generator.

Crying should be prescribed regularly.

Stoic, congested people can find momentary and often long lasting relief through the release of the tears.

Never send what you don't want to receive.

We can't healthily leave unless we are first able to develop the ability to stay. Then in many ways, if we are healthy, we leave.

When my friend's daughter was reviewing pictures which were all black and white, she asked, "When did the world become colorful?"

"When my son was born with Down Syndrome, I thought it was the end of my life, only to find out it was the beginning."

If anger is responded to with anger, we develop violence.

Many problems persist because the solution has no relevancy to the problem it is to resolve.

It's a long ride; pick a good horse.

Advertise that you are a victim and a perpetrator will find you.

Fisher people don't catch every fish; cops don't ticket every speeder.

Versatility is strength.

Make sure your veterinarian is also a taxidermist. Then either way you get your dog back.

Lessons from juggling: Don't fear dropping the beanbags; remember to let the beanbags go.

Couple therapy is over when a husband says to his wife, "The coffee is bad," and they both know you're talking about the coffee.—Paul Watzlawick

Loving freely is giving of your soul with only the hope that it will be respected.

Restlessness is bred from the belief that more can be done than what is currently being accomplished.

Contentment and complacency are not the same. One implies acceptance of engagement with the journey while the other implies non-participation with the journey.

Those who are spending their life searching for the meaning of life are missing the point.

Those who proclaim the truth are as confused as the rest of us.

If you're looking for God, He's easy to find. If you want to deny Him, that's more difficult and usually takes a personal loss.

A moment of appreciation can motivate hours of toil.

Criticism is the insidious disease that has caused the decay of the connective tissue between many good people.

Where is Grandma sitting in the room during our conversation?

Behavior is extrinsic before it becomes intrinsic.

Why didn't I end up like my sister? Because I didn't want to!

Some people talk to say something. Others talk to fill in the emptiness.

When the new relationship is better than the last, it is often not because of a better person but because of a changed self.

If you take my breath away when we're together and I can't breathe without you when we're apart, I'm in big trouble.

Many people drown in water that is only knee deep. It's best to simply stand up.

My resentment is about me, not you.

Cuss and swear or say a prayer.

Change forever? I haven't gotten to that point.

If it's a problem, schedule it.

Children learn to manage stress about as well as their parents.

When a problem persists, do the near opposite of what you were doing as an attempt to resolve it.

It couldn't have happened to a nicer person—except a few others.

WHAT IF?

What if the human race never evolved? Would we have world peace?

What if the Jewish faith is right and the Messiah is still coming? What is He waiting for?

What if there was no tilt to the earth and no seasonal changes? Would people still live in Minnesota?

What if there was a law that there could be no laws?

What if everyone practiced Christian values consistently?

What if there was a bounty on bad guys?

What if humans had gills and lived in the oceans? Would land be the challenge of outer space?

What if eagles are really alien spies?

What if there was never a continent drift? Would there be more or less peace?

What if we could truly feel the feelings of other people? Would we be nicer to them?

What if schizophrenics are really on to something?

What if after death we go back to our planet of origin?

What if love is only a figment of our imagination?

What if hate, bitterness, greed, and envy were not humanly possible?

What if all personal decisions had to be made through the thoughts and feelings of others?

What if the sense of sight never existed?

What if there really are vampires? Would you like to become one?

What if our thoughts could be read by others? How would we treat each other differently?

What if you had identity theft and amnesia on the same day?

What if there was an epidemic of global amnesia from which no one was exempt or could recover?

What if money was a perishable item?

What if you truly are created in the image and likeness of God?

What if the least of your brethren really is God?

What if the only gas we could use was what we could produce with our bodies? Would our diets change?

What if the only means of transportation was skipping?

What if you could only keep what you could carry with you?

What if no two politicians could be in the same party?

What if politicians truly represented their constituents?

What if politicians took a vote from their constituents for every vote they cast?

What if we went to heaven every night for directions?

What if meanness could be surgically removed? Would it be a requirement to have it removed to live in some communities?

What if imaginary friends are real?

What if we really believed that we get back what we give 100 fold?

What if children were fully grown and mature within three years?

What if we really are assigned a personal guardian angel?

What if only the less fortunate could take vacation trips?

What if the political opponents to politicians who support gun rights were allowed to be armed during conventions?

What if all negative, uncomfortable memories were erased once a week?

More Random Thoughts

The last mile of a marathon, as the last semester of 26 semesters, can be the most challenging.

Are you better off with or without your spouse?

Puppetry teaches the puppet what is really important to the puppeteer.

People respond to respect and resist power.

Rainy days are worth it if you can hear the rain drops from your bed.

It's tough to get away from the phone when it's strapped to your belt.

If you want to meet God, He's probably your most challenging neighbor.

If I could live my life over again, I probably would make more mistakes.

Poker is more addictive if you're chasing.

Marriage counseling and divorce counseling are similar. Both processes empower people to change.

If I eat healthy and don't drink beer, I may live until I reach 94. If I eat whatever and drink beer, I may live until I'm 90. I may forfeit the four years, eat well and drink beer.

Some people spend hours selecting food as they shop, hours cooking and hours eating. Others are too impatient and eat peanuts with beer.

I tend to not see what I see but rather what it could be. I drive realtors crazy.

Tragedy does not necessarily become traumatic.

Everyone has a story of significance.

Mom's wheelchair became Dad's walker. If Mom got better she feared Dad would fall. If Dad got better, he feared Mom wouldn't get around.

The only African phrase I worked at while in Mexico was "hakuna matata," meaning "no worries."

When you can't be in control, become curious. It's easier to be curious.

Silence and secrets can cause much damage yet when brought to light have a chance to heal.

The idea isn't bad, it just isn't me.

When you cry, it's okay if your eyes leak.

Non-conformists conform to non-conformity.

Non-prejudiced people who demean prejudiced people are quite prejudiced.

Dependency is like gambling with money you can't lose.

Lying can be very selfish; blunt honesty can be even more selfish.

Emotion is difficult to text.

If you strive to be a perfectionist, it's best to do it perfectly.

In order to stay in the poker game, you must fold your hand most of the time.

You don't need to thank people for them loving you. Just love them back.

Enjoy your memories. Don't live them. Live the moment.

Chronic venting is best if the listener is on meds.

You don't have to be the best player to be part of a winning team.

The best part of marriage is having to work at it.

A teen told me that their favorite Christmas gift is being with family.

The most open minded people are under the age of two.

Mother Teresa loved people with her smile.

Thank your wife half as much as you thank your waitress and your wife will be thanked seven times an hour.

Most people don't have hardware problems. It's their unwillingness to upgrade their software.

Talk to your younger self.

Get to know what your tears are really saying.

Smooch in front of your kids.

Anyone can do well when things go well. It takes a skilled person to do well when things are tough.

One way of knowing what others want is knowing what they give.

Change is made best by exaggerating it.

The gravitation pull of a rut is intense.

"How do you want it done?"
"Perfect would be fine!"

When kids are sick they can be more manageable.

No need to brush your teeth if you let them rot out.

ADHD is the "Ooh! Shiny!" disorder.

"I can't trust my husband because he dated other women before he met me."

People are imprinted to come back where they were raised.

Nursing homes are often the waiting rooms for heaven.

Being an adult is making your own choices and dealing with the consequences of those choices.

If God didn't forgive, it would be a hell of a situation for all of us.

It's not what happens to you, but how you respond to what happens to you, that make the biggest differences in our outcomes.

If you don't learn from the past it may just be a waste.

Feeling alone when you're alone is not as bad as feeling alone when you are with someone you love.

It is through tragedy that we become truly human.

Predicaments are problems with solutions. Problems are predicaments without solutions.

The outcome of exposure of children to diversity is measured by their initiation of diversity as adults.

Always have sunshine in your heart.

A very common request of teens in therapy is more time with family.

When you say it out loud, you own it.

Healthy people are strong enough to stay calm in times of adversity.

I've learned to enjoy them rather than judge them.

If you're not free to leave you're not free to stay.

We learn to live through death.

Get better—damn it.

The older I get the better I was.

I'd rather be disliked for who I am than be liked for who I am not.

Life may not have a meaning but it's up to each individual to find a purpose.

You can't leave home unless you've been there.

It's not a question of whether you can—it's how bad you want it.

Grief and relief are siblings.

Let your heart be the manger for Jesus.

I cherish aloneness; I dread loneliness.

Letting go of control is one of the greatest challenges of life.

Making a change only for the benefit of someone who is detrimental to you becomes detrimental to society.

Transitional people are like parachutes; once we land we cut them loose and move on.

I'm an individual; don't make me a herd.

It's not as fun to watch a game that you know the outcome of; it's fun to be curious.

Confidence is developed by facing your greatest fear.

Argue to understand, not to change.

The issue is not the differences, but how the differences are handled.

The Bible is a book of ideals and directions, not a book of demands and ultimatums.

Most emotional issues have something to do with loss, security, comfort and significance.

Show me your friends and I will show you your future.

I would rather be naively trusting and wrong occasionally than be naively paranoid and right occasionally.

Commitment works better than love sometimes.

If you fill your life with memories it will always be full.

We are catalysts in our relationships.

Foreplay begins in the kitchen and family room yesterday.

Once forgiven, never bring it up again. Always remember the lessons.

Change happens in an instant; it takes a lifetime to practice.

What can I do to enhance my desired outcome with you?

Everyone needs a friend who will not be offended when you fart.

Decisions are best judged by what history writes about them.

Age doesn't make people wise—wise people seldom act old.

Boundaries are built not on outcomes but on expectations.

Relationships don't last just on love.

I love all my children equally. It's just that some are easier to like than others.

Healthy mourners have a morning.

One problem of being a human is the continued desire to move forward while not wanting to let go of the past.

I'll have a good life in spite of your behavior, not because of your behavior.

A measure of personal strength is the ability to deal with adversity.

Be adult enough to handle rejection.

Untested values are simply concepts.

Maturity is the ability to postpone gratification; faith is the ability to postpone gratification until eternity.

Become unconsciously competent.

Walls are built on the foundation of a hard heart. Walls crumble when our heart softens.

Most couples need a handful of connecting points to succeed—five on one hand, five on the other, like fingers touching and igniting passion.

"Mommy, if I don't get any Christmas gifts, can you stay home?"

Everyone has a degree of optimism and hope, for without it we would not see tomorrow.

"You have been so nice and kind. You're wonderful to be with," she said. He began coming out of his shell. "Not like the asshole you always are," she explained. He climbed back in again.

Life has choices. What I once believed I could not do, I did. What I didn't want to do yet felt I should, I chose to do. What I wanted to do, yet knew the negative consequences of, I walked away from. Those who said I can't, I proved wrong.

I trust you enough to say I don't trust you.

People who choose to die are not those who don't want to live, but don't know how to live.

Optimism is the belief that people evolve.

Without hope we are simply waiting to die.

Most of the greatest joys of life occur in time frames of moments.

When we do our best, we live without regret.

The greatest diamond fields are found as the sun rises over rippling water.

Why is it that we are oblivious to so many of the beauties of life until someone we love notices them?

Hope allows the insignificant as well as the desperate behaviors to have purpose.

Ice boating makes sense if you like adrenalin, feel invincible and aren't afraid of death.

It was 16 years before I discarded my dad's collection of nuts and bolts and screws and nails and whatever else he saved, for I thought, as he did, that someday I would have a use for them. Even then I hesitated. I gave them to my neighbor.

Few things seem shorter than life as you get older. Few things linger longer than life when you're in pain.

After drinking dark beer, drinking light beer is like eating spaghetti without sauce.

I talk to my folks almost every day. They have been dead for years.

Best friends are people who enjoy what you have in common.

When I was younger a good day was when an adrenaline rush was normal. Today a good day is when calm is normal.

Buying a bigger boat only makes sense from the seller's perspective.

Proclamations from the mountain top may be made anywhere there is a mole hill.

At age 60 I told a 13 year old it was tough getting old. He agreed.

The best place to be is okay. Great is exhausting and poorly smells bad.

There will be as many good people in heaven as there is supposed to be.

I done it lists are possibly more effective than *to do lists*. Both are helpful.

Don't sweat more than your client.

Only God can make miracles.

A good therapist is like a good placebo.

Your emergency is not mine.

See a miracle every day. They are numerous.

If I could be someone else I think I would stay me because no one else is good enough.

I'm all in with one eye on the exit door.

It's not that I don't trust you. I don't know you.

Everyone could do better. We all settle. Settling is part of serenity.

We pay a price for comfort.

Peace can never be attained through violence.

Most people would support the philosophy of righteous justice. That's the definition of jihad. The questions are, "What is righteous?" and,"What is justice?"

There is a positive intent for all behavior.

If you don't know an answer, then create an answer that gives you the greatest comfort.

The greatest advantage of living in an affluent country is the freedom of choice.

People are basically the same.

The cost of comfort is some uncomfortableness.

People live in houses; families live in homes.

Our future, rather than being defined by our past, is defined by our present.

To be valued is our greatest motivation.

Blaming the past for the present is the greatest deterrent of a meaningful future.

People treat us according to how old we look. We often behave as old as we would like to be. It's best to act your age.

A bad attitude is a poison that we can choose or not choose to ingest.

Mentally mature people take responsibility for their own thoughts, feelings and behaviors.

Acceptance of our acceptableness is the process of self-respect.

Feelings are temporary

Play as hard as you work.

Only respond to who you are, not the name someone may call you.

Why should I go to his funeral? He's not coming to mine.

When you're an only child you don't have anyone to fight with at your parents' funeral.

"I choose to live with him to compliment my life rather than to complicate my life."

Lenz's Law: The induced current opposes the charge that caused it. Example—resisting God.

Idealizing the real can be more gratifying than realizing the ideal.

Life is not so humorous if you don't see the humor of yourself.

The other 'C' word, curious, works better than control.

Don't tie the skunk to the bumper of your car.

Healthy grieving is releasing; unhealthy grieving is recycling.

The greatest control is to remain calm in chaos.

The challenge of therapy is to challenge your tendencies.

Therapy is reviewing a person's life which to them is chaotic and overwhelming, and perceiving it in such simple terms that they can actually enjoy it.

If I need to medicate to continue doing what I'm doing, it may be best to quit doing it.

It's arrogant and grandiose for humans to think that we are the only intelligence in a universe so immense that there are dust clouds 80 million light years wide.

We create the glue of comfort which bonds us together.

"It's sad but what can I do?" is a philosophy that allows us to get up tomorrow.

"My heart's not ready," is not an excuse but an explanation.

Even a broken clock is right twice a day.

Live every day until eternity instead of dying every day until death.

Loneliness is the uncomfortable side of aloneness. Solitude, in appropriate doses, can be the comfortable side.

People are catalysts to happiness.

Depressed people tend to be self-focused.

Respond rather than react.

When jumping ship the swim is highly significant.

From solitude we see the big world.

If I always question whether the decision I made was the best, I'll never be comfortable with the one I made.

Life is too short to worry about what you think.

If you want to see Christ, look in the mirror and in the eyes next to you.

Some families are so low, even the dog is depressed.

Don't fight blizzards—just wrap up in a blanket.

Vacations are planned irresponsibilities.

We don't always agree with people we love.

Could healthy married people be married to any healthy person?

Avoiding discomfort diminishes growth.

You're this small; I'm this tall. I'm taking the high road.

People may agree that your idea is good yet your expression of your idea can be done so disrespectfully that it is utterly rejected.

Some people are smart enough to not have to learn the hard way.

Every week has a Monday.

It's my fault that I'm doing as well as I am.

Keep going until you get there.

Keep pedaling until you get to your luggage.

Indian summers are gifts from God as an expression of His gratitude to those of us who dare inhabit His north country.

Silence is the medium through which your soul speaks to your intellect.

Explain to me again why God, Who is omnipotent, allows children to suffer?

The greatest demonstration of resilience and expression of hope is in a child's healing from trauma.

Behind every gift there is a giver.

Faith says more about who you believe than what you believe.

Smart people are the ones who learn from the mistakes of others. The rest of us learn the hard way.

The war is over—let it be.

Would we have economic stability if all people services were of equal value?

Is there such a thing as factual news?

What's wrong with creating new words when playing Scrabble®?

What's the point of cheating when you play solitaire?

Why does it only take eight steel wheels on a locomotive to pull a mile long train but it takes 10 tires on a tractor to pull a semi-trailer 40 feet long?

One of God's greatest creations is that of the artist.

If birds were human, what would they change about their lifestyle?

Our greatest sins are those of overindulgence in ourselves.

If all the energy of wars and competition throughout the history of the human race was directed toward peace and human dignity, where could we be today?

The greatest tragedies bring about the greatest compassion.

People cluster in communities in response to our social nature and then proceed to kill each other.

If love flowed like a river, the people at the bottom would be the greatest recipients.

I wonder if the Twin Cities are identical.

If humans could fly, would we have airports?

Storms are God's way of telling us who is in charge.

If you feel a need to lie, it's wrong.

Acceptance and respect have much in common.

Pick a date and do it.

It's best to be a turtle if you're in a hail storm.

If mom couldn't change him, neither can you.

You cannot see in the dark without a glimpse of light.

The destination is the journey.

Healthy change is a different kind of normal.

She doesn't hate you as much as she would like to.

A good indication of how a person deals with people is how they get along with their parents.

The most placating women of the world are the most disrespected.

The goal is not to become more of what he wants but to be more accepting of who he is.

The more we accept people as they are, the more they become who we want them to be.

Getting to know your birth parents allows you to appreciate all of your parents more fully.

If your antidepressants aren't effective, try a placebo; according to some, they work a little bit better without the side effects.

A woman's attractiveness can produce as much pain as it can provide opportunity.

Create thoughts that serve rather than entertain thoughts that victimize.

Age makes no difference as a veteran.

I can walk on water when it's frozen.

I'm not afraid of death—I'm afraid of dying.

If you keep shoving things under the carpet, the bulge will get so big you're likely to stumble.

We can express our emotions with our non-verbal behaviors. We can create emotion with our non-verbal behaviors.

Every kid needs an advocate who is more powerful than they are.

If I'm living for you, I lost myself.

Some suffering is inevitable; misery is optional.

A healthy psychology has a healthy theology; a healthy theology has a healthy psychology.

Anyone can get along with cooperative people; it takes skill to get along with difficult people.

Flowers are weeds we like.

Snow people are cowards–they leave when things get hot.

Just because:
- People can be difficult doesn't mean they can't be enjoyed.
- The sun sets, doesn't mean the day is over.
- You're a mom doesn't mean you're a maid.
- You're a man doesn't mean you don't cry.
- A person has insecurities doesn't mean they're all true.

When boys have raging hormones, girls need a rising knee.

Happiness is an inside job.

Serenity can't be scheduled.

Peace cannot be attained by war.

People know the truth in their hearts.

Without optimism there is no hope.

Most people don't change until they're hit over the head with a brick bat.

The foundation of a wall is a hard heart.

It's not what's wrong with you but what happened to you.

The person who knows how will always have a job; the person who knows why will always be his boss.

If you are resourceful and powerful you will not be traumatized.

Terror is fear in the face of helplessness.

Rage is anger in the face of helplessness.

Resilience is vulnerability in recovery.

In tribal times, if men froze they would die; if women didn't freeze they would die.

Rituals are accepted behaviors that bond people together.

People become who we tell them they are.

What we give our energy to grows.

Distinguish between power and force. Power is demonstrated by empowered people. Force is demonstrated by those who feel powerless.

Force produces resistance; power attracts.

Kids do what parents do. If you don't follow through they won't either.

You don't have to do anything.

Kindness and a smile will always win more cooperation than grumpiness and a bark.

Going to a good therapist and going to a Catholic confession are similar in that both are confidential, require an understanding of what happened, have a plan to make change and result in people feeling much better. I believe God is involved in both.

What is the allure of living near water?

Families are changed by trauma. Some are torn apart through the intense emotions of blame, guilt and hopelessness. Others are bonded together through the sharing of understanding, forgiveness and hope.

If we had some eggs, we would have eggs and ham, if we had some ham.

If Mom and Dad were here today, they would both be smiling.

Calm water is often stagnant.

If heaven is like most days, I'll be quite pleased. If it is like today, I'll be delighted.

God expresses his kindness in innumerable ways. One way is through friends.

Sunrises and sunsets can be distinguished by the direction you face. The outcome of a marriage is similar.

Technology allows people to be in contact without being involved.

Some people are like the sun in that they are appreciated more when they are coming and going. Things often get heated in between.

Not shaving for a day is like breaking a minor law—you got away with it and no one was hurt.

A good football game can be enhanced by a small wager.

We have five rules when we travel with my sister and brother-in-law:
1. Warm
2. On water
3. Out of the country
4. Never the same place
5. And we can change the rules whenever we want.

I wonder what God thought when He heard the big bang.

If I were a fish, I would like to live in the Sea of Cortez as a whale shark and entertain curious people.

The most useful function of a cap is to hide an ugly head.

Do masochistic people lose at poker more often than sadistic people?

If you want to watch a football game, stay at home and watch it on TV. If you want an experience, go to the game.

People who enjoy brewing beer typically like drinking beer. People who enjoy drinking beer don't necessarily enjoy brewing.

Did Calvin ever grow up? I wouldn't mind having his little red wagon.

Are Hobbes and Puff together now? What about Calvin and Jackie?

What would the human race have evolved into if no medicine of any kind was ever utilized?

I can't control the wind but I can adjust my sails.

When you take bread from the loaf do you go back a few slices and take a fresh piece and leave the stale bread for your family? Do you take the best looking banana?

Chasing money on the poker table is like chasing a rabbit with a carrot–it typically doesn't work well.

"Pay it forward" works in most situations, but not in poker.

Patience is virtue especially in poker.

Being ADHD and a professional poker player do not necessarily blend well.

What's the explanation for the most intelligent creatures on earth taking the most time to grow up?

If death is so bad, why do people keep putting themselves in death's path?

If death is so bad, why do we go to war?

If you don't bet, you can't win.

I'd rather be led than pushed.

Leaders teach others how to succeed.

RAGBRAI isn't a race–it's a party.

How did I live through it? Childhood that is!

Your dreams have a message.

Sail the wind you have.

If you're a professional gambler, you end up spending a lot of time with losers.

Use your brain for a change–to make a change that is.

I wouldn't recommend walking on thin ice if you like to be grounded.

Playing poker on a tilt is like harassing the police; eventually they will get you.

Recording history is to categorize past perceptions.

How can news be new if it already happened?

Is there such a thing as past or future news?

If birds couldn't fly would they still get up so early?

Art is an attempt to recreate what God has already created.

Self-esteem and health-esteem have a lot in common.

Determine who you are by knowing those you love.

Treat yourself as your best friend.

Think about what you want, not about what you don't want.

Not thinking green is possible only if you do not think about what you're not to think about.

One of the greatest travesties throughout history was the belief we were victims of our environment. One of the greatest evolutions is believing we are no longer victims of our environment.

Kids with positive self-esteem can meet their needs more consistently with positive behavior. Kids with low self-esteem can develop positive self-esteem with positive behavior.

Blessed are those who are flexible for they shall not be bent out of shape.

Teens in trouble often have someone taking care of them and therefore can postpone growing up.

There is nothing wrong with getting high—it is how you do it.

Stress is a response to a perception.

If you don't like me, you don't know me very well.

If everything was blue we wouldn't see much contrast.

God is everywhere.

How do undesirable situations persist and what is required to change them?

Shifting gears often works better than giving it more gas.

I would be a somebody, if only . . .

If you can't write it, it is not clear enough.

Act; don't talk.

Change means something different to clothes than to humans.

They teach me more than I teach them.

I can't have a future until I let go of my past.

The past is interesting but I'd rather live now.

If you need a man to be happy, you won't be. If you are happy without a man, you could be happy with one.

A portion of bla*me* is me.

Prayer changes me, not God.

If your heart is open it can never be broken.

People resent those whom they depend on.

Forgive the dead. Forget the details. Remember the lesson.

If you can't measure it, you can't manage it.

All situations have seasons.

Motivation implies the desire to finish whatever was disrupted.

It drives me crazy that life is short.

It is not what you like about someone that makes a relationship work, but accepting what you don't like that makes it work.

The truest meaning of communication is the response elicited, not the response intended.

If you don't believe in the magic of words, try telling your boss, "You're nuts!"

The rules of Christianity are as simple as the rules of the childhood game, "Follow the Leader."

Kids do about as well as the parent who does the best.

What the courts decree is not as important as to what you agree.

Coaches have more influence than many parents.

Living in the past is cheaper, but not very satisfying.

Most things that are nice are not necessary.

Tell others what you feel and what you want.

"How are you doing?"
"Better after you give me a hug!"

The most uncomfortable part of a root canal is the thinking part before it happens.

Comfort is more important in a healthy relationship than excitement and drama.

No one is at fault but everyone is responsible.

We know what our futures are because we create them.

Dating is a prearranged, positive experience.

What would you do if you had human limitations with no ramifications?

I will consider your opinions when I make my decisions.

Wisdom is the ability to see things from many different points of view.

The day you feel comfortable on a motorcycle is the day you die.

Don't carry books around with you. Put them in the library.

Intelligence is the ability to learn. Change is the ability to learn something new. Intelligent people can therefore change.

Life is a paradox.

Openness heals. Covered wounds become infected.

Make a decision between both right and wrong, smart and stupid.

People get married so someone can witness their life.

If you hang around Italians long enough you will speak some Italian.

Have the courage to be imperfect.

Have the courage to be almost perfect.

Enjoy where you are rather than feeling guilty for not being where you think you should be.

If I focus upon what I did not get to do in my life I won't enjoy what I get to do now.

The most powerful animal in the world is a duck because of its versatility.

Stimulus-cognition-response works better than the stimulus-response-cognition.

Our country was settled by a lot of unsettled people who were diagnosable as ADHD.

Parenting a teenager is like being a dog. Be there when they need you.

Little Miss Muffet sat on a tuffet, eating her curds and whey. Along came a spider and sat down beside her and she beat the hell out of it with her spoon.

Relationships can be painful yet essential for living.

If you are told not to think green and you remember what not to think, you will not be successful.

We need the future to let go of the past.

It is a challenge to get past the past.

The challenge of the Temple of One Thousand Demons is to continuously move forward and face your fears.

There is a positive intent in all behavior even though all behavior is not positive.

The problem is the solution to the problem.

Attitude determines the degree of enjoyment of life.

Fear has no place in love.

Guilt is what I feel when I want to do more of what I did without feeling so guilty. Remorse is what I feel when I no longer want to do what I did.

Good advice from self to self: "Grow up, suck up and get over it."

Anything you do, if the words "I love you" come through, will be effective.

Anything different is better than more of the same.

If it ain't broke fix it anyway.

Time off for maintenance is always better than time off for repair.

The identical twin brothers, Omar and Oscar, were a team.

Preventing is better than fixing.

Healthy relationships grow through an awareness of alternative means of accomplishing positive ends through difficult moments.

Anger is an emotion we feel when we feel powerless and helpless.

Violence is a response to the feeling of powerlessness and helplessness in order to regain the feeling of power.

Junk yard dogs aren't mean, they're just scared.

Wit is the humor part of intelligence.

Sarcasm is the angry part of humor.

If you get up an hour earlier each day you will have an additional nine work weeks of vacation each year.

Anyone can sail in calm, steady wind. Skilled skippers can sail through storms and still get to their destination.

If one person changes, the system changes.

One cannot join the culture without changing the culture.

As a family therapist my client is a relationship. My goal is to help change the patterns of behaviors within the relationship.

Insight is nice but not necessary.

The goal of therapy is to discontinue ineffective cycles with the belief that people will develop more effective ones.

Our future is what we decide it to be.

We are the authors of our dreams.

Misbehaving teens have often declared a moratorium on growing up.

Misbehaving kids are often discouraged kids.

We tend to resent the person to whom we submit.

"Bad" behavior is the result of discouragement in the pursuit of significance.

As a parent, it is important to distinguish among the adjectives sad, bad and mad.

Significance is a primary goal of humans.

People are more motivated by desire than driven by fear.

There are several "f-words" in response to stress including fight, flight, freeze, fake, flourish, and fold. Food is a possible one also.

Compelling futures are the motivation of success.

Live life with passion and compassion.

Be both firm and gentle.

Be fair yet generous.

Success breeds success. Lack of success can breed success.

Responding to negatives is allowing black magic to change you. Responding to positives is allowing miracles to exist.

Persistence is more effective than aggression.

Steady growth is more positive than sudden gain.

I would rather fight a gang with knives than a ghost.

People who choose to change after long hardships with others are often welcomed with the "Son of a Bitch Syndrome."

We tend to marry someone different than us and then spend the rest of our lives attempting to make them more like us.

The qualities that attract us are often the very ones that become the most irritating.

Cybernetics is a significant process in any successful endeavor.

Death is not to be feared but to be prepared for. Don't be afraid of death; be curious about the experience to come.

Life has value because of its existence, not because of its longevity.

Our life has value because we exist, not because of our accomplishments.

Validating our worth is to question the value of life.

We discover our greatest strengths in the most vulnerable people.

The focus of therapy is the development of a more comfortable, optimistic and effective future rather than the continuation of an uncomfortable, pessimistic and ineffective past.

Generosity is giving to yourself through others.

Snow people are more like real people than we care to believe.

What we portray physically is frequently a disguise of the person we really are.

We may be what we eat, but we become what we think.

Mind over matter can keep you warm in chilly situations.

If you don't mind, it doesn't matter.

Integration of a person's life and death with your future is the most important step in grieving.

The ability to give is a primary aspect of love; the ability to receive is essential to the process of love; the ability to appreciate completes the process of love.

One cannot truly love without being vulnerable.

Patience is a virtue but so is getting the lead out of your ass.

There is love, true love, and then just putting up with your shit.

I would rather have a best friend than a good dog.

Dogs are like children who never grow up.

People used to go on vacations to get away from the phone. Now they bring their phones with them. Why go on vacations?

Explain again how fighting for peace brings about peace and harmony?

We sometimes use our perception of morality to justify insanity.

What if they had a war and no one came?

If your religion is a source of anguish and confusion, you are going to the wrong church.

Paradise is where you take your mind.

I may suffer to do well. I may suffer yet do well. I do not do well because I suffer.

The good fortune for heavy smokers and drinkers is that they don't have to save for retirement.

The greatest challenge for a good therapist is to help normal people uncomplicate the simple things they get all screwed up.

Acceptance is the anecdote to frustration.
If you don't want to become confused, then quit thinking about it.

People who manage stress well will make the most money.

If anyone can accomplish anything so can I.

Dreams are the beginning of our reality. Reality is the fulfillment of our dreams.

God is quite accommodating. He will be Whomever and Whatever we make Him out to be.

If I could live my life over again I would probably make the same decisions I made the first time because I would fear if I didn't I wouldn't end up where I am and I like it here.

There are no mistakes, just decisions that did not work out as well as anticipated.

We end up exactly where we put ourselves with our minds.

We can change history because history is a perception and perceptions can change.

Realities are what I perceive them to be.

TV is a plug-in drug for many and possibly causes more deaths from inactivity and obesity than any of the illegal drugs.

If you think the mission to outer space has been a trip, just wait for the mission to inner space.

Sea glass is what happens when God recycles our garbage.

We become a spectator when we want others to do, not what we wish we could do, but when they do what we wouldn't do.

I hope that the early Christians eventually got what they deserved.

I hope no Catholics went to hell because they ate meat on the Friday before they could eat meat on Friday.

I wonder what day most human beings would say was their happiest day on earth.

Children who have never grown up often have parents who have never grown up.

The beauty of art is that it expresses the beauty of the artist.

All people are artists. Professional artists are the ones who want to sell it.

If you have a flower growing out of your head, water it.

Sarcasm can be humor used competitively as a hurtful weapon.

If kids were taught to cooperate like they are taught to compete, we would have had world peace rather than football.

If music soothes the soul, then what is rap?

Music is the stuff I enjoy; noise is what the generation younger than me enjoys.

If you want to feel insignificant, go to the beach on a stormy day. If you want to feel significant, go to the beach on a stormy day and know that God loves you.

The importance of organized religion is to help people come together to help each other. It does nothing for God. He's got everything already.

I like my drive to and from work most days because it gives me time to get ready for what's next.

Most people spend their lives as if they are looking down a straw. The world really is bigger than that.

Living in the past is like living your life looking in the rear view mirror. You tend to hit things in front of you which makes the journey difficult.

If God is love and if He is everywhere then we don't need to look for Him in all the wrong places.

Love is never forced. Love is always free

When we walk the beach picking up shells are we missing the point?

Is a day without ice cream still a good day?

Can professional athletes play ball or do they have to work at it?

If God knows all things, does He tell everyone else up there everything also?

The more people available, time allowed, and money allocated for a job, the less efficient it becomes.

The most productive people are those who profit directly from what they accomplish.

Supply and demand is influenced most directly by attitudes and beliefs.

You never really enjoy the game of golf until you have walked the course barefoot.

Those who have the least going on in their lives often talk the most.

The more possessions people have the more they seem to need to enjoy life.

The ride from the top down is more painful than the ride from the bottom up.

Those who are most defiant of rules seem to live with the most rules imposed upon them because of their defiance. Many live in prison.

Most problematic behaviors were initiated as a solution to a problematic situation.

God can be seen in all things if you want Him there.

Many of our routine behaviors are conditioned responses to environmental cues.

All systems have a pecking order.

Those who are most effective in their role at the top of the pecking order are those who enhance the positions of those lower in line.

We become most anxious when it seems to be most important that we stay calm.

There are few physical differences between the states of anxiety and excitement.

It's difficult to love someone that you don't know; it's difficult to not love someone that you truly know. It's difficult to hate someone that you don't know; it's difficult to hate someone that you truly know.

Mental health issues are more learned responses than biological glitches for the majority of us.

The more we had, the more we have, the more we believe we need.

Healthy people smile more.

Religious people are not necessarily spiritual; religious people are not necessarily nice.

Life is easier if you have rules to live by.

Transparency in the moment is good for relationships.

Openness may be more harmful than helpful.

Accepting your responsibilities is a necessary step in the process of change.

There is a major difference between honesty and openness.

Constructive criticism is still criticism; positive, useful feedback is more effective.

Why is it that we thank a waiter/waitress more often in an hour than many spouses thank each other in a year?

Good coffee is really good; bad coffee is really bad. Good whiskey is really good; bad whiskey is really good.

Prayer is the expression of honor, thankfulness, gratitude and hope.

If we could do it all over again, we would do it all over again because we usually keep doing it all over again.

Patience and good timing are more effective than aggression.

Your important stuff is what you put in your suitcase when you go on a trip.

People become jealous of success.

Anger is the quickest exit from a relationship; calmness is the quickest entry.

Are you a prisoner or a refugee?

The greatest consequence of any misdoing is knowing that I am loved in spite of what I did.

Effective teachers learn as much from students as students learn from their teachers.

When we feel bad, we often do what makes us feel worse. When we feel good, we do what makes us feel better. If when we feel bad we did what we do when we feel good we would feel better.

What we say to ourselves is more influential than what happens to us.

At one time in my life I would have been with anyone rather than be alone. Now I'm much more selective.

Ever Wonder?

Ever wonder what those who believed the earth was flat thought was beneath us?

Ever wonder what people would be like if coffee wasn't discovered?

Ever wonder how the world would be today if electricity was not an option?

Ever wonder what people did before mental health counseling?

Ever wonder, if people laid eggs would we eat them?

Ever wonder, do birds have mid-air collisions?

Ever wonder who you would be if you had to choose to be reincarnated?

Ever wonder how messed up the human body would be if humans were to be in charge of creating one?

Ever wonder what day in the past you would choose if time were to stand still?

Ever wonder why you got to be a human rather than a worm?

Ever wonder what would it be like to be your spouse? Your child? Your employee?

Ever wonder, do state and national governments buy lottery tickets?

Ever wonder why gangs and packs of dogs act so much alike?

Ever wonder if dreams are reality?

Ever wonder why animals don't need supermarkets?

Ever wonder what auto body repair people would do if there were no deer?

Ever wonder how different our medical system would be if prevention was the only option?

Ever wonder what the population of the earth would be if antibiotics were never developed?

Ever wonder what the population of the earth will be if new antibiotics are not developed?

Ever wonder what one natural food you would choose if you could only eat one thing for life?

Ever wonder how the world would be different if alcohol and drugs were never developed?

Ever wonder what would happen if cooperation was addictive?

Ever wonder, do tragedies occur to bring people together?

Ever wonder, does God really talk to us?

Ever wonder, does God present Himself in your most difficult neighbor?

Ever wonder, did Jesus date as a teen?

Ever wonder if Jesus was an athlete today, which sport He would play? What position?

Ever wonder if Jesus was in a band, which instrument would He play? What song would He sing?

Ever wonder what Jesus would do if He were you for one year? How would things be different at year's end?

Ever wonder how different your life would be today if you had the challenges of the person you dislike the most?

Ever wonder how you would be different if you were the parent of you?

Ever wonder how many people would show up for a bullfight if they had to feel the pain of the bull?

Ever wonder why parents are arrested for hitting their kids yet they can allow them to play football?

Ever wonder what would you put in your suitcase if it contained all of your worldly possessions, had to be under 50 lbs. and contain no currency?

Ever wonder, does capitalism without compassion work in the long run? Is that what we have?

Ever wonder, is democracy without compassion the beginning of decay?

Ever wonder, should we move to Prescott, Arizona?

Ever wonder how much disease is transferred on money?

Ever wonder how much disease is transferred because of money?

Ever wonder what your life would be like if all major decisions had to be completed by the age of fourteen?

Ever wonder why you survived childhood?

Ever wonder how the world's population would be distributed if there were no sources of heat? What if there was no air conditioning?

Ever wonder if our families are closer or more distant because of cell phones?

Ever wonder if TV reality shows are about real life, why don't they show people watching TV on TV?

Ever wonder, if this life is to prepare us for the next life, what life skills are we to be developing?

Ever wonder, do healthy people smile more because they feel good or do people who smile more stay healthier?

Ever wonder what you would have changed about the constitution if you were to write it today?

Ever wonder what you would tell Columbus if you could talk to him the day before his discovery of the new world?

Ever wonder how our country would have developed if we had lived by the values of the Indians?

Ever wonder what you would be if you weren't born?

Ever wonder why is flute music so relaxing?

More Random Thoughts

Few experiences are more cozy than a chilly, foggy day with nothing needing done.

Alcohol and poker are seldom a good mix. Poor decisions become too costly.

It would be difficult to be my sister. For that matter, it would be difficult to be my wife.

If you want a sign that God exists, use your senses.

Patience is a component of most success stories. I pray each day that God will give me more of it right now.

I may never retire, therefore it would be best to enjoy life now and act as if I am retired with so many meaningful activities keeping me busy that I don't have time to think about not being retired.

If I needed to be a fish, I would like to be a dolphin. If I needed to be a mammal, other than human, let me be a squirrel. If I needed to be a bird, I would prefer being a duck. I would hope I wouldn't need to be anything else like a worm or an insect. I'm grateful to be a human.

Few emotions are more crippling than fear. It produces despair and abandonment of one's dreams.

Although it takes a team to lose a football game, I still say a prayer for the player who made the last mistake that allowed the other team to win.

If you went to a movie and you didn't laugh or cry, it was a waste of your money.

If you went to a movie and you left scared or angry, it was a waste of your money.

Don't ever leave a movie without learning something about your emotions.

When I was younger, I occasionally enjoyed inviting lots of people over all at one time. Now I enjoy inviting a few people over lots of times.

It was a good date if you laughed often.

I spend way too much time on airplanes.

The most important goal of life for a kid, young person, and even people as old as a parent, is to learn to enjoy the gift of life.

Life is a gift with many options, like a Rubik's Cube®. It is up to us how we adjust it.

All life has value. The attempt to validate our value is perhaps one of our most detrimental behaviors.

Don't let another person's sin destroy your joy.

It takes strength to get through.

Peace is the softening of what is rigid in our hearts.

The simplest things in life are the most complicated.

The secret is to accept others as they are.

Never tell a father that he is obsolete.

We all have a purpose—it just changes. Old roles are replaced with new ones.

Divorce can be like a civil war and the enemy is your spouse.

You evolve into what you gaze upon. You evolve in the direction of your focus.

"I never made a wrong decision because I always did what my parents said. And they were always right. And that's why I am here today," said the client to the therapist.

I have the right to be angry but not the right to be aggressive.

There is a lot of anger in the word d*anger*.

Love is magic.

Bug zappers prevent us from being bugged.

It is better to be an anthropologist than a missionary, especially with our family of origin, in-laws and siblings.

The most successful people focus on successes not yet accomplished physically, but that have already occurred emotionally and intellectually.

You can't join a system without it changing; most systems won't let you join if your goal is to change them.

We tend to love God less than we love our neighbors and we tend to love our neighbors less than we love ourselves. It is best to love ourselves a lot.

You can't give away what you don't have.

Beliefs direct our thoughts. Thoughts create emotion. Emotions generate behavior.

Human software is called an operational belief system.

Confident people make mistakes.

Positive people excel.

To be successful, focus on successes—past, present, and future.

Life is a series of choices. Some choices soar like an eagle, others quack like a duck.

Don't steal from others. Let others own their feelings and responsibilities for their feelings.

Don't cheat people; let them experience the consequences of their own behaviors.

Find the good in every situation.

People are enormously forgiving and tend to forget the negatives.

My goal is to do good.

There are no shortcuts, but there are a lot of detours.

A wild and crazy lifestyle may be fun for the day, but in the evening it tends to be lonely and sad.

Love is doing what it takes to assist the one you love to feel loved.

Love is a verb.

Love means wanting to say you are sorry.

If you love someone and they don't know it, they don't benefit much from the experience.

Don't worry about the future because God is already there.

We all live in a shack. It is up to us to make it a loving home.

Don't ask the question if you are not ready to handle the answer.

A secret of happy relationships is to become more like the person you love rather than to expect the person you love to become more like you.

Effective families are polylingual.

Allow what you want to be more powerful than what you have. Allow your future to be more influential than your past. Allow dreams to be more inspirational than reality.

What you want is more powerful than where you have been.

Blended families don't grow together, they collide.

Building a relationship is like blending two trains and railroad tracks into one, combining the cars, and each person taking responsibility for a rail. The more ties between your rails the more secure your track and your train.

The more connecting points you have in a relationship the more stable it becomes, similar to the ties on a railroad track.

Healthy people attract healthy relationships.

The number one reason for failed marriages is emotional starvation.

The "inability" to trust often says more about the feelings of inadequacy of the one not trusting than about the non-trustworthiness of the person not being trusted.

The more secure we are, the more capable we are of forgiving.

More violence is caused by despair than by anger.

Marriages are both work and a miracle.

Be more affected by the future than by the past.

Love and spirituality have a lot in common including faith, hope and charity.

Learning to get along with the enemy includes getting to know how they feel.

Loving your enemy has a lot to do with self-acceptance.

You have to love you to love others.

Anyone can deal with the good times; it takes skill to deal with the bad times.

I am the way I am because of my past; if I stay that way it's because of me.

I can change now regardless of where I was then.

Romance influences fighting more or less.

Fight like it is a lecture—let one person talk and the other can ask questions to better understand.

My present is more determined by what I want in the future than by what happened in the past.

Is the plaid shirt white with red and blue or red with blue and white?

No one should be owned. No one can be controlled.

The greatest human freedom of all freedoms is the ability to choose how you feel.

Feel sorry about the things you can control—feel sad about the things you can't control.

I don't know my mission in life. I just go around and do my thing.

Good guys may not always follow the job description. Not-so-good guys might.

When the dust settles we often realize that nothing has changed.

Bucket lists are not to get you ready to die but to allow you to live.

Anyone can get you through the easy times—only successful people get through the tough times.

Some people have to go to work; others get to go.

Acceptance is not only accepting the reality of a loss but also the reality of a future.

Violence is the result of believing you don't have a choice.

War is two-year-old behavior initiated by adolescents.

If parents could have felt the feelings of their kids today in the past, they would have been better parents then.

If kids conceive their future in their present, they have hope. If kids conceive their past in their future, they are discouraged.

The sun shines even though there are clouds. Enjoy both.

Everyone likes a warm spot to go to in cold environments. Furnaces are nice.

Evolution is inevitable. How we evolve as a society is a choice.

Some of the most painful choices result in some of the most pleasant outcomes.

If a thought gives you problems, create a new one.

Use emotion to determine the effectiveness of thought.

Fighting a child is like fighting the wind; you will never win.

Fighting like a child will get you nowhere if you're involved with healthy people.

When you do something unforgivable remember to forgive yourself.

Always have something in the hopper.

We are attracted to those who speak our language.

If you grow up in Italy you speak Italian. If you grow up in France you speak French. If you grow up in anger you speak anger. If you grow up in love you speak love. If you grow up with dope smokers you smoke dope.

Don't ask a question if the answer won't help you.

"I don't care" is a great attitude in regard to many things.

Effective parents are like oak trees. Raising teen-agers is like being oak trees in a wind storm.

Rough weather makes good timber.

Learn from the past—don't live there.

Not having options is like being on house arrest.

Options are like insurance policies. You have them with the hope of never having to use them.

What do you hope for as you make change? What do you hope for as you live? Is there a difference?

We are able to live when we are ready to die.

People often begin to live when they are out of time.

People build walls to see who will tear them down.

People live inside of walls not to keep others out but to keep themselves in.

The greatest fears are generated not by others but from my lack of understanding of others.

Drive your own bus.

Life is a lot like driving. If people follow some very simple rules, most of the time it can be an enjoyable experience.

The difference between me with sleep and me with no sleep is the difference between night and day.

The difference between me with positive thoughts and me with negative thoughts is the difference between light and dark.

I don't have a future until I accept my past.

Chronic depression is often the result of being depressed because you are depressed.

Schedule your depression. It is similar to going to a support group or taking a shower but I would not recommend you live in either place.

The past has not been so good for me so why do I keep going back there?

It is not a question of good or bad; it is a question of effective or ineffective.

If the past did not get you where you want to go what will you do now in your future that will get you where you want to be?

The past isn't good so why are we here again?

My past made me who I am but it doesn't stop me from becoming who I want to be.

Some people have a personality that they like to have but don't want those hanging around them to have.

Forgiveness is the ability to see it through another person's eyes.

The most Godlike thing a human can do is to forgive.

Living is making one memory after another. When you quit making memories you no longer have a life.

Life is like a marathon; we often hit a wall that if we don't overcome will stop our run.

The final stage of grieving is acceptance.

Reality is what I perceive it to be.

Trying to make sense out of nonsense will drive you crazy.

There is no such thing as try.

Healthy people become intimately comfortable with uncomfortableness.

What gives you the most comfort today may give you the greatest pain tomorrow.

Healthy living is the result of conscience cybernetics.

To remain effective, make the unconscious conscious.

Synergistic energy is way more powerful than willpower.

Few good things ever happen alone.

Isolation is one of the worst types of self-imposed imprisonments. Solitude can be one of the greatest pleasures of life.

Skin contact is more important than sex.

Sex without a relationship is overrated.

God was no dummy. What good would an extra rib do us men anyway?

There is a God.

It is better to focus on the successes of the future than the mistakes of the past.

Mistakes are to be learned from, not focused upon.

Think of mistakes as decisions that did not work out well.

The greatest challenge of children is to resolve the conflicts that their parents were unable to resolve.

If you are not challenged you get soft.

Victimization is often self-imposed.

The disease to please is sad and can also be terminal.

I am not what I anticipated to be, yet I became what I wanted to be.

Your heart is the foundation of your walls. If you soften you heart, your walls fall down.

The major difference between Catalina Island and Alcatraz was the freedom of transportation.

Love yourself with rocks in your shoes.

"It's not that I don't care. I'm just tired."

Some parents do the best they can. Some should have been neutered.

If my parents know so much about parenting, what happened to me?

Wearing your cap backwards makes sense if you want to be different from your parents.

Stopping emotion is like stopping the rain. Let it storm, enjoy the shower and occasionally use an umbrella.

Forgiving is the easy part of forgetting.

Honor your life by forgiving yourself.

Our past is more influential because of our emotional responses and the effectiveness of our coping skills than because of the realities of the situation.

Poker is not gambling if you play the odds and listen to what your opponents are telling you.

If you have a carrot in your nose and a banana in your ear then you are not eating properly.

One-trial learning experiences adequately teach most people. Some people, however, require more training.

Three percent of us are simply difficult. The other 97 percent are quite likeable.

Anyone can live in a paradise. It takes skill to live in the North Country.

Success can be lonely.

The best things in life are free but often come with a price that we are unwilling to pay.

If you are average or above in intelligence and you are motivated, you can do anything.

Emotion is like urine. Hopefully you will find a proper time and place to release it.

Don't fight the wind—just let your sail out temporarily.

Fire drills prevent hot issues from becoming destructive.

Schedules can be lifesaving.

There is always time for the important things.

If we work 40 hours a week and sleep 60 hours a week, what do we do with the 68 hours left over?

Mindfulness is non-judgmental acceptance of the living present.

Effective grieving involves remembering, resolving and integrating.

Never get over things; get through things.

Life is simple but not easy.

Therapists spend their lives making problems into predicaments with solutions; their goal is to make the complex simple.

The goal of a parent is to become obsolete yet valued.

OCD is an art form.

Healthy people have strong convictions and are curious of yours.

Trusting is naive.

Naivety is an essential quality of healthy living.

What do you hope for as you make changes?

Life is tough. It's even tougher when you act stupid.

Why does the house next door have their windows closed?" she asked. "No one lives there, Dear," he responded.

Dreams initiate goals. Goals are achieved through action steps by someone who believes themself to be worthy. If you don't believe you are worthy you will prove yourself right.

Fashion is out of hand if you trip over your shoes and they happen to be on your feet.

When I play poker it bothers me more if I play my hand poorly and lose than when I play it well and lose. It doesn't bother me at all if I win.

If you are the only one who benefits from your endeavors they are probably not worth pursuing.

You are the director of the film of your life.

Living on the edge is the way to go if you have a railing and a lifeline.

Healthy adjustment to a major change often takes four seasons.

The greatest guitar player I ever knew practiced daily in order to continue to be the greatest guitar player I ever knew.

Real men cry.

Feelings are to be felt.

Why would I want to kill someone who doesn't want to die any more than I do?

I have not hunted since Vietnam. The killing just doesn't seem the same.

Opportunities are never lost. If you don't find them someone else will.

When consulting about your ethics always begin with the phrase, "I have a friend who . . ."

I am best at guessing distances under a foot. I can usually be within six inches.

To succeed in any organization it is helpful to develop the fine art of kissing ass.

The situation is hopeless, but not serious.

When you are curious about a statement in a book, call the author.

Every relationship has a control issue.

People who guilt trip have too much power or a lack of it.

The greatest leaders are not known to be so.

The only time I feel like sleeping is when it is time to get up.

When I stand by the ocean I experience the paradox of feeling so insignificant yet so significant.

Love yourself with lots of issues.

Be a like a duck, not like a sponge. Both float on the water. Both go to the bottom. Ducks come back up.

Sister Martin, my first grade teacher, was wise. When I couldn't sit still in class any longer, she would have me clean the chalk erasers that hadn't been used since the last time I cleaned them.

They lost their house but they found their soul.

If you don't put it in your suitcase when you go on vacation you don't need it ever.

An error often made with children is to respond to them rather than to lead them.

I would rather struggle for something than be challenged by nothing and grow nowhere.

The opposite of love is apathy.

If my choice was to travel with a woman with a dog or not travel, I would choose to not travel.

If my choice was to travel alone or stay home, I would stay home.

The excitement of travel is great, but not as significant as the comfort of returning home.

The greatest differences among people are the perceptions of themselves and the way they manage stress.

One of the greatest discomforts of traveling in countries where you do not speak their language is not knowing what people are saying about you. I experience the same sensation while shopping in most major shopping malls.

Music is an emotional stimulator; expressions are mood initiators; attitude is a behavior creator.

Music at unwanted times is noise.

When going to the airport I'd rather be an hour early than a minute late.

The more I travel the more I appreciate picture signs.

People should be required to travel with each other before they become business associates. In a matter of days you can gain years of insight.

Why do clouds seem to be more beautiful from above than from below?

Have you ever seen a mid-flight collision of birds? Thank God humans can't fly.

Coffee is the drug of choice for the sleep deprived.

If you ever want encouragement to have children, observe families who are traveling with kids. If you ever want discouragement to have children, observe families who are traveling with kids.

Skinny people and fat people grocery shop differently. The skinny ones buy what they need on their shopping lists after lunch, while the fat ones buy what looks good before lunch.

If we watched as much TV as people we watch on TV watch TV we wouldn't watch much TV.

Why is it that the urge to pass gas is greater when in enclosed spaces with others?

I think that Tourett's Syndrome among fathers of little league players is more common than we know.

If I want to be entertained I don't want to watch movies where people die; I want to watch movies that make me laugh.

Cities are best for people who don't know what it is like to not live in the city.

Ever watch people preparing fast food while wiping their noses with their plastic gloves?

I bet your most memorable college experiences have little to do with academics.

I live in Iowa. My favorite seasons are the one I am currently enjoying and the one that is about three weeks away.

If all the people in the world who have adequate food would fast one day per week and could give their food to a starving person, there would be no starvation on earth.

If all people lived like Americans, the Earth would have been destroyed by global warming around 1910.

Why do good girls like bad boys and bad boys like good girls?

The absence of sound can be noisy.

Yawns, laughter and fear are all contagious.

There is nothing more healing than a hearty laugh and a great lover.

Dreams can take you to where you enjoyed being, prepare you for where you want to go, or take you back to where you never wanted to be.

Optimism is the greatest economic stimulus investment.

Life in the fast lane has a lot of bridges out because they have not been built yet.

Living life vicariously is like picking your nose with someone else's finger.

You can learn a lot about people by the way they eat.

Life is like flying—it is the taking off and landing that can be the most delicate and emotional.

The ability to cat nap allows you the joy of avoiding some of life's most uncomfortable situations.

Early morning is the time to enjoy life before people clutter it up.

Having cousins is like having friendships you didn't have to earn.

Most dogs make better parents than many people.

Kids will live within the limits adults set and are willing to enforce.

If I had a penny for every blessing I have received in my life, I truly would be the richest human being financially. Without the pennies I still would be the richest human being with my blessings.

Why is it, while visiting the developing countries of the world, it is I who feels like the poor man?

If you want to feel selfish, look around you.

I once thought, "What could I think that others haven't thought?" And then I realized, "Everything."

Successful people are those who do the things that unsuccessful people don't want to do.

The most successful people are those who choose to be happy.

Living alone helps you appreciate living with others. Living with others helps you appreciate living alone.

One of the best birth control methods known to teens is a daily hug from their dad.

Some of the greatest motivation in life is observing the success of others.

Life appears manageable from the windows of an airplane. Reality sets in when you assess the damage to your luggage at the airport.

I once heard that people who eat fast food daily consume an average of 23 ounces of other people's snot and mucus per year. Enjoy your meal.

Sleeping on an airplane works about as well as sleeping in a Volkswagen® with eighteen other people. It is difficult to get comfortable.

Why did God create the housefly with such maneuverability? Think of the possibilities if we could sit upside down.

When people are willing to trade homes with you for vacation, maybe it would be worth asking them what they would be doing while they are in your home and then stay home and do those things.

Sometimes we have to leave the forest to appreciate the trees. Sometimes when we leave the forest we realize how protected and narrow our lives have been.

When people just go with the flow they seem to go downhill.

When people say, "Keep your head up," they are typically not implying your ass.

If you believed everything you were told you would have quite a challenge defending your beliefs.

Values are beliefs that are lived.

Living is what we do when we forget what we were supposed to do.

Try means you will do it if it is comfortable.

If sexual energy could generate electricity we would truly be an enlightened species.

Not doing something until your feet are firmly planted too often implies the grave.

If today is the tomorrow of yesterday just what does the repair man mean when he says, "I will be there today"?

I can think of numerous places where I would enjoy living. I can think of no place where I would like to live more than where I am.

Having a strong faith is like having an instrument certification while flying an airplane. The certification may not seem necessary when the skies are clear, but it can get mighty cloudy up there.

One of the greatest limitations of personal development is to focus on what I cannot achieve because of my past rather than on what I am willing to do to achieve my goals in the future.

Successful people are often working in a different time sequence than those who don't succeed. Successful people live in their future and learn from the past, getting them to the present. Unsuccessful people focus on their past to justify why they can't move from the present to have a better future.

The longer the vacation the greater are the comforts of home.

Diversity is like light; we become brightest when all the races are blended.

The feeling that I have been there before becomes more profound the more I travel.

I don't believe in reincarnation, but if I must come back I would prefer to come back as me.

If you think you have it bad, just imagine the people who have to put up with you.

Eighty-five degrees and sunny may be nice, but I'd rather be in 10 degrees and cloudy with someone I love.

What some people do once they are successful is what some unsuccessful people do every day.

True success is the ability to serve.

A day with a purpose is better than a thousand days with no point.

A day without an agenda is like living blind with no white cane.

A sailboat can sail around any coordinates. It is important however, that the coordinates be in water, there is adequate wind, and she is equipped with a good skipper.

I left Puerto Rico when it was 90° F and flew to Minneapolis where it was 3° F and I liked it better. What is wrong with me?

Before you pronounce someone dead it is best to check to see if they're not just tired.

The older I get the more I appreciate and understand the characteristics about my parents that I did not like.

Ever wonder how cartoonists would characterize you if you became famous? Perhaps that is why you did not become famous.

Ice is water's way of taking a nap.

How would we live differently if we acted upon the belief that all life has value?

What you think is what you'll get.

We touched. I heard you breathe. Thank you, whale.

Part of the allure of traveling to a foreign country is the challenge of communicating without speaking their language.

The poorer people are, the less likely it is that they will discard their garbage.

Maybe animals get along better with each other because they don't talk so much.

What is the entertaining part of violence?

If I lived my night dreams I would have one very confusing life.

What percent of the earth's hard surface is privately owned? Will we ever begin buying acres of water surface?

I think I could tour the world on a bus only if the windows were clean.

If money did grow on trees, I bet trees would be quite scarce.

Imagine the economical affect if no one mowed their lawn for one year. I wonder what other obsession we would develop.

Suicide is an act of impatience.

The enjoyment of life can be diminished by thought.

Getting high is what you do when what you do has little meaning.

Sleeping your day away may be worth it if you have great dreams.

If all religions went to war, I fear the Amish would lose.

If we lived as the Amish, there would be no war. If people of all religions lived their faith, there would be no war.

A little food will go a long way if you have little food.

The complications of living a simple life may be more difficult than it's worth.

Knowing you will be here tomorrow brightens up today.

The most beautiful spot in the world is where you are.

If you could spend one day with an ancestor you never met, who would it be? What would you ask if you could only ask one question?

The garbage in foreign countries seems to be more colorful than garbage back home.

I touched a whale once. She touched me back.

Sunrises and sunsets are even more beautiful if you share them with someone you love.

True love can see beyond the flaws; true love is also strong enough to process the issues.

The most memorable moments in my life were when I was touched.

Together we fight; alone we cry. Maybe a piece of you would be just right.

The people most bothered by control freaks are other control freaks.

If people drove cars the way most people drive golf balls, we would all be in the ditch.

We are all alike in life and death, but I like the alike in life better for now.

I wonder what I would say to my family if I had an opportunity to state my final words. I don't think anything profound. I think I would simply say, "I will always love you."

A frustrated artist is a person who thought what could have been created needed to please others and therefore stiffed him/herself.

If I knew that my siblings would become my best friends, I may have gotten to know them at a younger age.

When you talk for a living, you tend to be quiet when you have time off.

A good cup of coffee does more for me than a good beer. That's why I drink more coffee.

Knowing where I'm going allows the process of going to have more meaning.

It's not good to be intimidated by your doctor, lawyer, therapist, or investment broker.

She never liked to be around Susie because then she wasn't the prettiest girl in the room.

If you truly look for God, He will appear everywhere.

Tennis is a good game for young people and for those who like to think they're young.

I thank the sea lion that bit me because it makes such a great story.

Spirituality is not found where you live; it is found how you live.

I do not need to become a monk to have a relationship with God.

In order to leave home we need to have already been there.

I can't let go of what I don't have.

Sacrifice is not to experience pain but to become less selfish.

My parents died many years ago; my relationship with them continues to grow.

I hope God isn't thinking about retirement.

Music comes in many forms. The sound of the sea is one of them. The laughter of my grandchildren is another.

Having no reason to get up each morning can be more stressful than the busiest schedule.

If I were to die tomorrow, because of today, I would not be disappointed.

The closest things to eternity are the sea and the sky.

Race, color, creed, age, nationality, language, sex, social status, family of origin, occupation, education—all of it is irrelevant. All people are good.

The ability to be oblivious to the stressors of life and enjoy the moment is a gift given to us from God.

Some of the nicest people have the fewest possessions. Some of the nicest people have more than most.

Some of the most honest statements are made after you drank one more than was good for you.

Everyone has a story.

Most of the people on vacation are similar to us. They come from somewhere similar as us, they do similar things we do while on vacation, and they feel similar about going back to where they came from.

It's possible to stay so busy that you don't meet yourself.

God was easy to meet today. I believe I meet Him every day in many places and in many people.

Silence may be golden; meaningful communication is mining it.

The more I travel, the more I miss family.

My most lonely feelings are when I'm with people who have detached.

The most difficult part of going back to work after vacation is not having beer for lunch.

After spending a month in LaPaz I realized that I hadn't heard an angry voice for a month.

People on vacation are often looking for friends; others want to get away from them.

The antidote to anxiety is, "I don't give a shit."

There are few things worse than watching an old film in a foreign language with poor earphones while on a turbulent flight.

Winter Olympics aren't very popular in Mexico.

When the coming home from vacation is as good as the getting away on vacation, the vacation must have worked.

Seeing more smiles at the Cabo Airport than at the Detroit airport had nothing to do with the airport.

Lack of trust in a relationship seldom is related to unfaithfulness; most often it is related to the feared response of your honesty.

Masochism is what you do when you accept your identity from those who resent you.

Solitude can heal the soul with peace or fill it with pain, dependent upon what is remembered.

It is the "out of the ordinary people" who help you with self-acceptance.

If I pass up this opportunity now, I will never have this opportunity again in my lifetime unless I'm reincarnated and fat chance of that happening.

Expectations are resentments waiting to happen.

Alternatives allow the current situation to be more acceptable.

A good day with a negative moment is like a sunny day with a drop of rain. A bad day with a negative moment can be like the last drop of rain before the dam broke.

If you are lucky you get one adulthood and two childhoods.

It is through the acceptance of differences that we become more similar.

If someone suggests that if you leave them they will make your life miserable, there is no loving reason to be together.

I have been so fortunate throughout my life. When another good thing happens to me I sometimes feel guilty, like I crowded in front of the line for good things.

The little white lie is likely to mature.

The power of hope is immense.

The ingenuity of people continues to be amazing as we strive to keep in contact when we are apart.

The greatest of obstacles can be overcome when people who are separated desire to be closer.

Being alone and feeling lonely is better than being together and feeling someone's resentment.

Getting drunk at a wedding is an insult to the bride and groom.

St. Paul spent more time in the epistles telling men how to treat women with respect than he did telling women to be submissive to men.

Healthy marriages demonstrate mutual respect and mutual submission.

Poker is more like real life than most people realize. The better I know you, the better I play the game.

Some firefighters become firefighters because they like fires.

People hurt themselves so their emotional pain can be physically expressed.

Living in a cave doesn't do much for the social skills of the average male.

Addictions are coping skills taken to an extreme.

We love our cats as they are, yet when our teenagers act like our cats we become extremely irritated.

Children are the perfect miracle of two imperfect people.

World peace may be accomplished if we would all go to sleep at sundown.

Sailing into the sunset could get awfully hot.

If you know who you are and someone calls you dumb, nothing changes.

If I know who I am and I'm called a name that I am not, I won't respond.

Be naively optimistic.

Waking up to parrots is more conducive to restful sleep than anticipating an alarm clock.

Any beer on the beach is good beer.

Life is more abundant than any of us can comprehend.

Not speaking the language of people we meet intensifies the awareness of those aspects of communication that cannot be verbalized.

One of the basic differences I perceive while working with others is the tendency of some people to do what they do to accomplish a goal, while the goal of others is to simply do what they do.

Is it true that the degree of one's relaxation is directly related to the amount of absorbed sunshine?

One of life's great frustrations is the necessity to accommodate the schedule of people who live with a different perception of time.

Birds that fly in formation such as ducks, geese and pelicans take turns leading the way and following behind. If people would do the same we could live in greater peace.

I began counting the different colors I saw from my patio and when I got to 100 I decided to quit counting and just enjoy them.

I understand there are numerous poisonous snakes where we are living. If I stay out of their home and they stay out of mine, I think we'll get along just fine.

People with low self-esteem have a fear of not being accepted. Those with high self-esteem have overcome that fear.

If you play tennis with a mediocre tennis player you play mediocre tennis. If you play tennis with a good tennis player your game improves. If you play golf with a mediocre golfer you play mediocre golf. If you play golf with a good golfer it just pisses you off.

I was the only English speaking person in the pool side bar overflowing with a mixture of nationalities and languages. Not understanding what was being said by anyone heightened my awareness of the experience in the present without the need to thoughtfully respond to what was heard.

I say today, with good health, that I would not do anything extraordinary to save my life, especially if my quality of life was diminished. I may think differently when the time comes to make those decisions.

Remembering the past with someone who hasn't lived the life events you have lived can be a frustrating and empty experience which may re-ignite feelings of pain that were once felt. Remembering the past with someone who has lived the life events you have lived, can be a healing, empowering experience which may re-ignite the feeling of ecstasy of survivorship.

It was a bullet ride.

Thank God I have the opportunity to take longer vacations. It takes me about a week and a half before I relax enough to recognize the change in scenery.

If your team loses the Super Bowl®, the best thing about the game is the food. If your team wins and the Kellers made the food, the food may still be the best thing about the game.

Laughter is a gift from God that sooths when all human initiatives fail.

There was a time that solitude was feared as the ultimate emptiness of life. As time evolved solitude was accepted as part of life. As life transformed, solitude was a pleasure frequently sought.

The power of the Internet is immense. With one negative blog about an excursion I was transformed from an excited potential traveler to a stay-at-home slug.

Comfortableness can be uncomfortable.

Do you get restless when you relax?

Fear is protection from other uncomfortable emotions.

Will there ever be a time when the inability to be active is desirable?

"My parents lived a long time and that is my wife's greatest fear of me," he said.

What will be the surest indication that we are dead after the event occurs?

We ate in the presence of one of the natural wonders of the world and we talked about our food.

It is much more satisfying to beat the arrogant poker player who thinks he can't lose than to beat the insecure player who fears he can't win.

One of the greatest joys of vacationing is finding the similarities among people and the contrasts in the way we live.

Few things taste better than a hot cup of black coffee in the morning and a cold glass of dark beer at night.

Humans are traumatized because of the incomplete transformation from reptile to spirit.

Peace is not achieved through giving to others what they want but rather through enabling others the opportunity of achieving what they want through their own efforts.

What is it that exists between the molecules of air?

We paid the fisherman more for one fish from his boat than what he got from the fish dealer for all his other fish. We paid him 20% of what we would have paid back home.

If the key doesn't work it is probable that you have the wrong key.

If you travel 4000 miles and do the very same things you would have done back home, you begin to wonder why you traveled so far.

When living in a colder climate you can layer more and more clothes to keep warm and stay comfortable. When living in a warmer climate there is only so much you can take off and you still sweat and suffer.

When she saw me, she jumped and screamed. I thought she was happy to see me. She said she was scared.

On a Sunday we drove through the rural areas of Panama and witnessed hundreds of Panamanians walking, many as families, many were teens. We witnessed no conflict, many smiles and no one was overweight.

Positive emotion broadens behavior; negative emotion narrows it.

Some of the prettiest songs come from the smallest of birds. The music sure makes them sound big.

There was a bird outside my open window that made hissing sounds like a snake. Even though I knew it was a bird, I closed the window anyway.

What's nice about sleeping in a room with several geckos and possibly other lizards is that you seldom get bug bites.

The sounds, smells and feelings of a rain forest are as beautiful as the sights.

It's best not to drink and drive in a foreign country, especially when you don't know the laws. It's not a good thing to do if you do know the laws.

If I didn't feel so responsible for taking care of people, I may enjoy them more.

Acceptance and appreciating are as different as having to go to work and living out your dreams.

Countries that have been traumatized by war have traumatized their children, who in an attempt to resolve their trauma as they grow older, will re-traumatize themselves through acts of war.

What I remember may make sense only to my body.

Remembering and emotionally sensing are often inseparable.

One of the obstacles of peace is that we treat others as we treat ourselves rather than treating others as we would like to be treated.

Furnishing a house with wood makes the house a home of nature.

Thank God for the people who are willing to accept their predicaments while they do the best they can in their situation. I hope God rewards them well.

Witnessing the landscape through a tinted windshield from an air conditioned vehicle deprives the senses of what they came to appreciate.

It is in the morning that every bird wants to be heard. It is then that they produce the greatest symphonies.

Cell phones have done as much to produce detachment disorder as convenient foods have done to produce obesity.

Flowers are God's way of saying, "Have a nice day!"

The Panamanian woman who cleaned our home was as proud of her work as any craft person I have ever met.

One of the indications of a developing country is the availability of safe drinking water.

Some cultures are historically peaceful. Others are historically violent. I think it has much to do with the traumatic experiences they have endured.

Some of the nicest, most open people you meet are those by the pool side whom you will never see again.

While I sit on the front porch my eyes dance with color.

In the States the inner cities are often populated by cultural groupings in an attempt to maintain their culture. In some of the progressive towns in developing countries the indigenous people move further into the country or down the beach in an attempt to maintain their culture.

We met a man in his home on Isle Boca Brava where he could see water on both side of his home as he listened to monkeys and parrots. He was there since October. We met him in February. He said he was unmotivated to do much of anything. Can life get too good?

It's been over three weeks since I left work. Without a project I become restless; with a project some say I become intense. I like the intense feeling more.

Life without purpose is not living; it's existing with the acceptance of the belief that there is no future better than what has been.

Exercise for the sake of exercise is difficult. Exercise in the process of accomplishment gives purpose to what is difficult.

I wonder how much electricity would be generated if every piece of gym equipment was converted to a small generator? We could possibly be both physically fit and enlightened.

Eating fish isn't worth it if you have to catch and filet it first. Let someone else enjoy the excitement of the catch and yet another demonstrate the skills of filleting. I'll pay them for their efforts.

Three months of any season is about right, if not a bit too long.

I often wonder if someday someone might enjoy reading what I write as much as I enjoy expressing my thoughts in writing for someone to read.

We investigate property each place we vacation, always with an ocean view, most often with a mountain and ocean view. Spectacular places exist in the world. However, we haven't found a place yet that compares to our home where we witness the blessings of spring, followed by the relaxation of starry summer evenings; we are enveloped in color throughout autumn and are transformed by blizzards in deep winter. I think we will stay home.

Comfortable emotions broaden behavior; uncomfortable emotions narrow behavior.

I seldom eat meat without thanking the animal that fed me.

Walking the beach during the rain storm washed away the tears of guilt felt for living in such comfort in a land of such poverty.

It is better to feel gratitude for what was given to me by the grace of God than to feel guilt because of the advantages that I enjoy.

Emotions, feelings, and sensing are as fundamentally different as intelligence, experience, and life.

Mandatory education for all children is one of the most effective means of improving the quality of life of those who live in developing countries.

When given the opportunity for a citizen of a developing country to live in the U.S., or for a U.S. citizen to live in a natural paradise area of a developing country, most people will choose to live where their loved ones live.

Most ex-patriots we met on vacation who are now residents where we were vacationing were escaping from someone or something.

The people of the United States, who leave our country because of the politics of the U.S., don't understand the process of democracy.

Moving to something is healthy; moving to avoid something can enhance discouragement to the point of despair.

Any environment is improved with the movement of air.

It is the variety of sensations, the diversity of the senses, the uniqueness of experiences, and the continuous change and variation of events that enables the truest appreciation of life.

Alcohol can intensify any given emotion. If you're upset, you become angry. If you're happy, you become entertaining. If you're tired, you become exhausted. If you're contemplative, you become eccentric. If you're narcistic, you become obnoxious.

Thank God for bugs—at least the ones that pollinate flowers.

If I was an artist I would thrust colors on a canvas signifying nothing yet providing a feast for my color thirsty eyes.

There is no object, creature, plant, element, molecule, or atom without predetermined form, structure, organization, and purpose.

There are few things more invigorating than un-expected, non-damaging storms.

I truly enjoy gourmet food if it is prepared by someone else.

Dealing with your emotions with people through avoidance is effective in minimizing the emotions while diminishing your quality of life.

A great restaurant has great music to accompany great food. A great bar has great music to accompany your dancing with friends.

People perceive life uniquely. The more similar the uniquenesses are, the more probable the unique-nesses will join rather than alienate. Stated more simplistically, the more we have in common, the better we get along.

While in Panama I swam a river to get back home. When I was in the middle I recalled the locals said there were alligators and crocodiles in the area. I swam the second half much faster.

I thank God for being with our children when we can't be there for them. I thank God for being with them when we are there, too.

Often my dream life is so busy that I need to wake up to get some rest.

People dream in themes. Some are doing some-thing, others are having things done to them and yet others are observers of what is happening. I'm glad that I am typically a doer.

When you live in paradise it is easy to take the comforts and the beauty for granted.

Why is it that the smallest bird in our yard, I believe a wren, sings the longest and most beautiful song? I'm glad I don't know what it is singing because I may not like the lyrics.

In paradise there are no major fluctuations in the seasons. The sun is consistently up at 7 a.m. and sets at 7 p.m. There is little to prepare in anticipation of a big change. I believe that is one of the reasons the paradises of the world are so often rampant with poverty. It can be done mañana.

Is it easier to pray in nature or is it that God makes his presence more obvious there?

The most difficult people we ever meet on vacation are often those who moved permanently from the States to get away from people who thought of them as the most difficult people they ever met.

Seldom do those who moved permanently to a paradise destination share about their families back home. I wonder what happened to them.

While on vacation out of the country it is seldom that we see an overweight local person. It is also seldom that we see a non-overweight vacationer.

A good breakfast isn't satisfying enough to justify the preparation and cleanup. The same is true of lunch and dinner.

What would the world be like today if humans had no more intellectual ability than a smart dog?

If it wasn't for birds we would need to listen much more carefully to enjoy the sound of nature.

The sense of responsibility can be as much of a curse as it can be a blessing.

If you see God in the person next to you, and that person happens to be me, please lower your expectations.

Humor, lived in our daily lives, is more typical and intense than is reported.

An unspoken thought may be profound; a verbalized thought may be judged with ridicule. It's worth the risk.

With the right frame of mind any statement can be viewed from a humorous perspective.

The positive of not speaking the language of where you travel is that you don't personalize their sarcasm.

Caring is both the cause and the cure of the uncomfortableness felt by those who want to do well for others.

Hope without work is just a dream.

Courage is a great virtue.

You're never too old to become someone new.

When there is a "Y" in the road take it; when there is a "!" in the road, take it also.

While on vacation I experience a wider range of emotions than while at work. Perhaps it is true that relaxation is a catalyst that allows expressions of the soul.

There were several palm trees in our yard the five weeks we lived in the tropics. They were for the most part ignored until the day before we left to go home to the snow.

Remember to appreciate the smell of grapefruit or garlic on your fingers after handling them.

Appreciation is the ability to recognize the blessings of your life that you have not earned. According to my calculations that implies I have much to appreciate.

Two parakeets flew over us today. They were more beautiful than the ones I've seen in cages. They seemed happier, too.

The advantage of not speaking the language of where you travel is that you don't have to work hard at acting dumb when you get questioned and you don't take feedback personally because you don't have a clue what they just said.

We get away on vacation to break away from the chains of routine only to develop a different routine which is similar to the old one.

The best hot sauces are the ones that leave your mouth burning for just a few hours.

Life is neither a race nor a competition. In my line of work I win only if you win.

It is impossible to grow without looking beyond yourself. Which direction you look and who you look up to will determine the quality of your growth.

Thank God we live longer than most animals because it takes us longer than most animals to mature. To some maturity means that we are developed. To others maturity means that we quit growing. I believe it means that we can live life more fully.

113 Thoughts about Healthy Living

People can evolve.
Skin can heal.
Always have alternatives.
Keep your hair short.
Life rules are simple.
Humans are social.
Face your fears.
Keep walking.
Walk. Don't ride.
Imagine beyond reality.
Make conscience effort.
Practice the 5 P's: Proper prior planning
   prevents problems.
Meaningful rules are mutually respectful.
Too much rain causes shallow roots. Too little rain
   prevents expansion.
Social skills are contagious.
A change of clothes does not change the person.
Understand the Law of Reciprocity—you get what
   you give to yourself.
People are doing what they choose to do.
Practice cybernetics—the science of self-correction.
Anchor your emotions.
Experience compelling futures—see it, hear it, smell
   it, taste it, feel it.
Recycle your positive past into new futures.
Repair yourself.
Have rituals.
Celebrate your successes.
Values and boundaries make life simple.

Have a goal of enjoying life.
Make gray black or white.
Focus on solutions.
There really is magic in words.
Life is a paradox.
What I have I don't need.
Absence produces a vacuum which is a forceful
    motivation.
Life is like a trip; it starts with a walk, bigger steps,
    a drive, a flight, a drive, and ends with steps,
    smaller steps, and a walk.
Start contagious positive behavior.
All behavior has a purpose.
All behavior has a positive intent.
We have immense powers.
We have the resources to do anything that others
    can do. Our challenge is to access those resources.
Consciously develop competence to become
    unconsciously competent.
In the big picture life is not logical but has
    divine order.
There is a God.
Have a purpose.
Forgive yourself and others.
Make decisions from first, second, and third
    positions.
Be the director of your own movie.
Everyone sells something.
You know your future because you create
    your future.
Look beyond yourself.
Make a choice, any choice.
Make decisions.
Think positively.
Do the opposite of tendency.

Eat the fresh bread if you are going to throw
part of the loaf away anyway.
Ask for help.
Pay it forward.
Grow with people.
Follow your own rules.
Stay focused.
Challenge history.
Change history by changing perceptions.
Shit makes the best fertilizer.
Emotion is like urine. It will eventually come out—
choose a proper time and place.
Make like a duck. Be versatile and let things roll.
Sail your wind.
Love yourself with rocks in your shoes.
You can get to any destination if you know where
you are going.
The principles of sailing apply to life.
Never dump sewage upstream from your
water intake.
What will future generations write about our
choices today?
Small changes can product major impacts.
Life without expectations is boring.
Mow your own lawn. It is cheaper than going
to the Y.
Do something different. Anything different.
Trust naively.
Dare to dream.
Write goals.
Help others.
Pray.
Look forward.
Keep your head up.
See your future.

Stretch boundaries.
Live in moderation.
Learn something new.
Love.
Have skin contact.
Enjoy a variety of activities.
Stretch and exercise.
Create.
Imagine.
Sing.
Make music.
Communicate.
Believe in something bigger than yourself.
Focus on what you want.
Listen to your dreams.
Respect your intuition.
Listen to your gut/heart.
Be attentive.
Give to others.
Accept help.
Second positions switch.
Anchor positives.
Sequence behaviors.
Physiologically edit.
Enjoy yourself and others.
Update your emotional information.
Challenge your morality and values.
Be open to challenge and conflict.
Get above it.
Be versatile.
Create challenge—personally, mentally, physically,
    and spiritually.

THE ALPHABETIZED LIST OF LIVING THOUGHTS

A Awareness of your God given worth.

B Believe in the impossible.

C Confidence to follow your dreams.

D Develop skills to maneuver toward goals.

E Efficiency is the way to go.

F Fantasy is the beginning of the future.

G Game plans are a prerequisite.

H Help others succeed and you will be richly
   rewarded.

I Inquisitiveness opens doors.

J Justice is living with love.

K Knowledge from those who preceded you.

L Levitate above the words that can be
   discouraging.

M Manage your life with the help of God.

N Now is the best time to act.

O Opportunities are abundant.

P Persistently work toward your goals.

Q Quality and quantity can coexist.

R Responsiveness to the situation that we are presented.

S Synergistic energy fuels the success of dreams.

T Teamwork makes the dream work.

U Utilize the resources of the universe.

V Visualize goals as if they are already accomplished.

W Wisdom is the ability to perceive many points of view.

X Xemplify the qualities and strengths of others.

Y Youthfully appreciate and enjoy each step as if it were the first.

Z ZZZ's cut at night make the days go better.

Marriage Thoughts

Marriage is a mutual admiration society.

If you like her, you can learn to love her; if you love her, but don't like her, it will be a long life.

Marriage is more of a business partnership than it is a romantic adventure.

Most of the challenging aspects of marriage revolve around the business of everyday living together issues.

The most common symptom in problematic marriages is emotional starvation.

When an irresponsible person enters a marriage, the arrangement typically allows him/her to continue to be irresponsible for a longer period of time.

A rude awakening for many is that rather than change people, marriage can entrench people in old patterns.

My wife once advised me, after three weeks of marriage, that if I thought I married my mother, I married the wrong woman. It was good insight.

Do troubled couples have more problems than other couples or do they simply focus upon them more?

What is so wrong with accepting and forgetting the irritating behaviors that tend to persist regardless of what we say or do?

I know my wife loves me with my positive idiosyncratic tendencies. I hope she can love me with my not so positive idiosyncratic tendencies.

A daily date is not too much to ask for.

Egalitarian relationships imply the acceptance of our equality with our unique qualities, abilities and differences.

One person always being in charge is as ridiculous as your partner always serving in a tennis match.

When things go well in your marriage, you are both responsible; when things go poorly in your marriage, you are both responsible.

If my wife were to have sex with another man or be emotionally involved with another man and not have sex, I would rather that she just have sex.

Problems are predicaments that have not yet found a solution.

Expecting someone to be different is the surest path to discontentment.

Wanting things to be different without the discomfort of reviewing the potential for personal change will only breed resentment.

We have a few choices in life. We can accept any given situation, we can change our response to any given situation, and we can leave any given situation. We don't have the choice of changing other people in any situation.

If I am in an interactive relationship with someone and I change my part of the interaction, the other person will also change their part of the interaction.

A positive change in a relationship is typically responded to with a positive change. When the response is not positive your decisions are still easier.

I would rather be in a non-sexual relationship with my best friend than in a passionately sexual relationship with someone I don't like. But then I'm not seventeen anymore.

If you want to see an ideal family lifestyle, watch the raising of goslings. Mom and Dad stay together with their youth until they are grown up. Then they all go on a long vacation together somewhere where it's warm.

If, when we married, we knew that our spouses would change very little in their behaviors, attitudes, beliefs and personality over the course of their lifetime and we were happy with them as they were, and if they knew the same about us, and they were happy with us as we were, people would be quite happily married.

If we would consistently enhance our respect and consideration of our spouse, we would have phenomenal marriages.

Marriages are like campfires that sometimes blaze, other times glow; sometimes they are highly functional, sometimes they are destructive; sometimes they are an allure. They, however, always need new fuel and need to be tended, especially in rainstorms.

Successful marriages are like a successful trip across the ocean in a sailboat. Anyone can sail in balmy weather; it takes skill to sail through storms. And it's best to know what to do before a storm comes. And it's nice to know when a storm is coming.

We've met hundreds of couples who live on boats. Most are glad to reach harbor so they can have some space.

Not letting go of past hurts is similar to not taking out the garbage and you had fish last week.

What you say is not as important as how you say it.

When you use bleach regularly expect something to be damaged.

There really is a difference between loving someone and being in love with them. There is also a difference between being in love with someone and being infatuated with them. Not knowing the difference can be heartbreaking.

If it takes drugs to tolerate someone, maybe the best medication is abstinence from the person.

If the drug you are addicted to is a person, abstinence may be part of your recovery.

If God is love and I love you, then God must be between us.

Commitment is what keeps us together when you're being impossible.

If I search until I find the perfect spouse, I'll waste a lot of time looking and probably end up back with you.

Having a great marriage says more about the skills of the partners than who the partners are.

It's easy to be married to some people; others seem downright challenging. Some people make great canoe and tandem bike partners. Others you wish you would have left at home.

Watching the behaviors of your future in-laws gives you a good indication of what your fiancé will be like as a spouse. Your fiancé either wants you to be very similar to their opposite sex parent or someone very different. Either way your fiancé will most likely be very similar to their same sex parent.

We tend to have a lot in common with the people we find most difficult to accept.

When I put you on a pedestal, the loneliness can be as great as what I feel when you put me on a pedestal. It's best to rock climb together.

I can't change you and you can't change me. Yet if I change, you will too and if you change, so will I.

It is such a paradox. It is when I don't need someone that I make the best partner and when I'm the most needy that my relationships don't work.

Marriages are like other professions—we practice them.

Very few things in life go well without balance and moderation.

An "I love you" genuinely sent and truly felt can erase much hurt. An "I'm sorry" genuinely sent and acted upon can be almost as effective.

One of the most effective interventions to improve your marriage is the commitment to not continue to talk about the problems from the past but about what you hope for in the future.

Twenty-one Final Thoughts for Marriage and Relationships

Always date.

Take personal responsibility.

Be comfortable with uncomfortableness.

Encourage personal growth and development.

Develop friends with similar values.

Teach your spouse how to treat you.

Maintain intimacy.

Schedule the important things.

Exercise random acts of love.

Schedule monologues/dialogues.

Appreciate differences/diversity.

Spend time with healthy couples.

Enjoy alone time.

Expect miracles.

Develop new/unique activities together.

Expect positives/catch positives.

Practice "No work" times.

Share projects, goals, and domestic responsibilities.

Balance "5 L's": Labor, Leisure, Love, Learning, and Laughter.

Make love a verb.

Pray together—put God in your marriage.